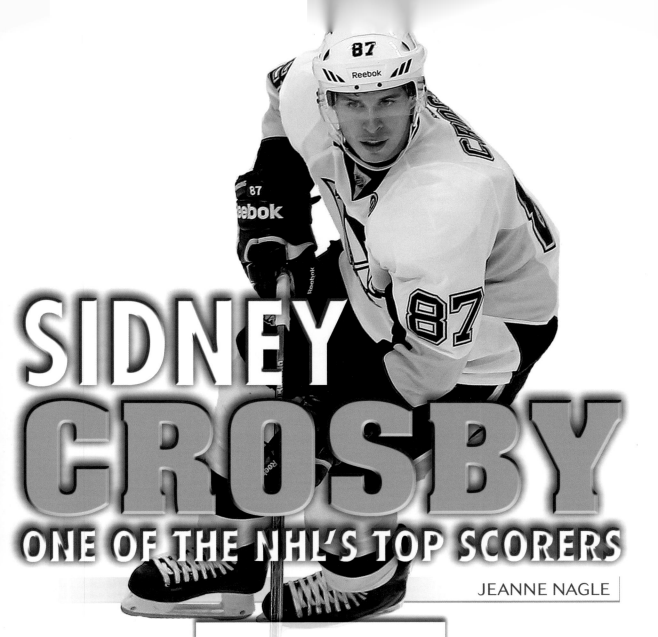

SIDNEY CROSBY
ONE OF THE NHL'S TOP SCORERS

JEANNE NAGLE

Britannica
Educational Publishing

IN ASSOCIATION WITH

ROSEN
EDUCATIONAL SERVICES

Published in 2016 by Britannica Educational Publishing (a trademark of Encyclopædia Britannica, Inc.) in association with The Rosen Publishing Group, Inc.
29 East 21st Street, New York, NY 10010

Distributed exclusively by Rosen Publishing.
To see additional Britannica Educational Publishing titles, go to rosenpublishing.com.

First Edition

Britannica Educational Publishing
J. E. Luebering: Director, Core Reference Group
Anthony L. Green, Editor, Compton's by Britannica

Rosen Publishing
Hope Lourie Killcoyne: Executive Editor
Heather Moore Niver: Editor
Nelson Sá: Art Director
Nicole Russo: Designer
Cindy Reiman: Photography Manager

Library of Congress Cataloging–in–Publication Data

Nagle, Jeanne.
Sidney Crosby: one of the NHL's top scorers/Jeanne Nagle.—First Edition.
     pages cm.—((Living Legends of Sports))
Includes bibliographical references and index.
Audience: Grades: 5–8.
ISBN 978–1–68048–124–2 (Library bound) — ISBN 978–1–68048–125–9 (Paperback) — ISBN 978–1–68048–127–3 (6–pack)
1. Crosby, Sidney, 1987– —Juvenile literature. 2. Hockey players—Canada—Biography—Juvenile literature. I. Title.
GV848.5.C76N34 2016
796.962092—dc23
[B]

2014040309

Manufactured in the United States of America

CONTENTS

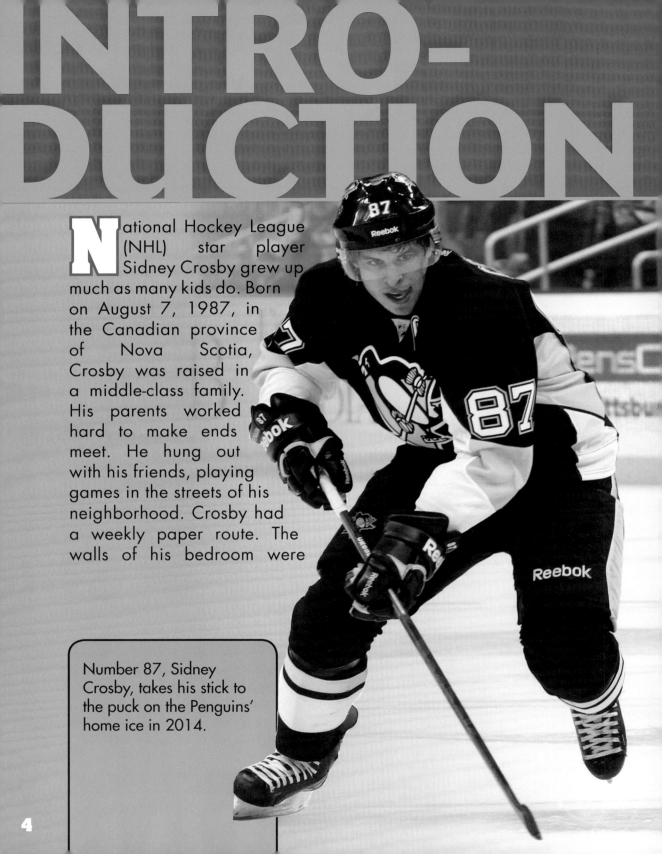

INTRO-DUCTION

National Hockey League (NHL) star player Sidney Crosby grew up much as many kids do. Born on August 7, 1987, in the Canadian province of Nova Scotia, Crosby was raised in a middle-class family. His parents worked hard to make ends meet. He hung out with his friends, playing games in the streets of his neighborhood. Crosby had a weekly paper route. The walls of his bedroom were

Number 87, Sidney Crosby, takes his stick to the puck on the Penguins' home ice in 2014.

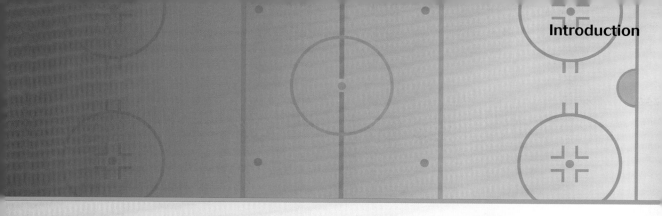

covered with posters of his sports heroes. And like millions of Canadian children (and adults), he loved the game of hockey.

In a few important ways, however, Crosby was different from other kids his age. For instance, he had fantastic motor skills that gave him an edge as an athlete. He started skating when he was three years old. By the time he was seven, he was playing hockey with kids who were twice his age—and giving his first newspaper interview about his success on the rink. One of those posters on his bedroom wall was of Mario Lemieux, a hockey superstar with whom Crosby would later live and work.

Crosby is nicknamed "the Kid" because he has achieved so much in the sport of hockey at such a young age. His fame and success have made it possible for him to do charity work that helps children in the United States and his native Canada. With practice, a great work ethic, and a true concern for other people, "the Kid" has grown up and become a living sports legend.

CHAPTER ONE

"The Kid" as a Kid

Some people might argue that Sidney Crosby was born to play hockey. Both of his parents had strong connections to the sport. His mother, Trina, had two older brothers who played. One of them was good enough to get a try-out for a minor league team in the Canadian Hockey League (CHL). Troy Crosby, Sidney's father, played in the Quebec Major Junior Hockey League—often called simply "the Q" by Canadians— for two seasons. The Q is a respected amateur league for hockey players aged sixteen to twenty. Although Troy was also selected as a goaltender by the Montreal Canadiens of the National Hockey League (NHL), he never actually played for the team.

Hockey is a family affair with the Crosbys. Here, Sidney (*far left*) poses with (*from left to right*) sister Taylor, mother Trina, and father Troy in 2010.

After he finished playing in the Q, Troy Crosby took a job as a facilities manager, in charge of the security and upkeep of a law firm's office building. The job helped the family buy equipment and tournament entry fees for Sidney, who loved playing hockey from an early age.

Denting the Dryer

In the Sidney Crosby collection at the Nova Scotia Sports Hall of Fame, there is a picture of toddler Sidney drinking from a baby bottle while holding a hockey stick. It seems that Sidney was drawn to the game even before he first laced up a pair of skates.

Also in that collection is a clothes dryer that is almost as famous as Sidney himself. When Sidney was a boy, Troy Crosby painted part of the family's basement floor to look like part of an ice hockey rink and set up

Crosby's intensity while playing hockey first resulted in a dented dryer. Later, he dented his opponents' egos as he channeled that power into scoring against them.

a goal net. When Sidney and his friends practiced making slapshots into the net, the missed shots often hit the nearby dryer. The poor thing was marked up and had its buttons knocked off, although it kept on working for years.

Because of his basement practices, Sidney got very good at shooting and making goals. A February 2010 *Sports Illustrated* article noted that Troy, who was a goalie in the Canadian Hockey League, had to stop guarding the basement net against Sidney's shots when the boy was around nine years old. Apparently, Sidney had gotten so good that Troy was afraid he might get injured by a flying puck.

Lighting Up the Minors

When he was five years old, Sidney began playing organized hockey with a team in Cole Harbour, his hometown. The team was part of the Timbits Minor Hockey program, sponsored by the Tim Horton's restaurant chain. From there, Sidney moved up through the levels of minor, or amateur, hockey in Canada. At fourteen, he was playing midget-level hockey, which is normally reserved for those ages fifteen through seventeen.

During the 2001–02 season, Sidney scored 193 points; 95 goals of his own and 98 assists where other players scored thanks to his passing. Those are impressive numbers for so young a player, skating at that level. His team, the Dartmouth Subways, went all the way to the Air Canada Cup, which is a national championship tournament at the midget level. The Subways came in second, but Sidney's style and level of play drew the attention of a national audience for the first time.

QUICK FACT

A local newspaper interviewed Sidney about playing hockey when he was only seven years old. Asked about his success on the ice, he told the reporter, "You have to do your best and work hard and things will happen. You can make it if you try."

A Place to Excel

At that point, Sidney was good enough to play in the major juniors, which is the level between the minors and professional hockey in the NHL. The trouble was that he was too young. Sidney had gone up against older players, called "playing up," for almost all of his time with organized hockey. His parents fought to get him into the major juniors, playing for the Halifax Mooseheads, but the league's management would not allow it.

Sidney could have continued to play in the Canadian minors, but his awesome skills had upset some people. Other players and their parents were tired of the attention Sidney was getting. Consequently, he was roughed-up on the ice and people shouted nasty things from the stands.

Because he had lost his bid to play for his hometown team in the major juniors and playing conditions in the minors were unpleasant—maybe even dangerous—Sidney decided to attend Shattuck-St. Mary's boarding school in the United States. The school is well known for its excellent hockey program. While there, he set many new scoring records. Sidney helped the school's team win the national championship in 2003.

Going International

The summer after winning the title for Shattuck-St. Mary's, Sidney had the opportunity to play for Team Canada in the Under 18 World Junior Championships. Sidney scored six goals over the course of the tournament. Although his play was impressive, Team Canada came in fourth overall.

Stepping out into the international spotlight only drew more attention to this up-and-coming hockey star. Hockey legend Wayne Gretzky was asked if he thought anyone would ever break the many records he had set during his

THINKS our CAPTAIN is SID-SATIONAL

CANADA

Sidney has made a splash on the international scene. But as this young fan's sign shows, Canadians are always proud to claim him as one of their own.

time playing in the NHL. Gretzky answered, "Yes, Sidney Crosby." He went on to say that Sidney was the best player he had ever seen play the game since another hockey great, Pittsburgh Penguins center Mario Lemieux.

QUICK FACT

Sidney has had a number of nicknames in his career:

"The Next One" A reference to his being the next best player after Wayne Gretzky, who is known as "the Great One."

"Darryl" In honor of NHL player Darryl Sittler, who has the scoring record of ten goals in a single game; recognizing Sidney's great scoring talent.

"Creature" Supposedly because his teammates think his legs and butt are so muscular and developed that they are monster-like.

"Sid the Kid."

Fit to Play

Sidney studied and played at Shattuck-St. Mary's for only one year. Still, his time at the boarding school was important for many reasons, one of which is that is where he first started working with strength trainer Andy O'Brien.

Even though he played hockey very well, Sidney wanted to improve his game. He recognized that he wasn't a very fast skater, and he needed to work on his speed. The family hired O'Brien to get Sidney in excellent physical shape. They worked out three times a day over that first summer, concentrating heavily on increasing Sidney's speed on the

A bird's-eye view of Citadel Hill, where Sidney performed strength-training drills in Halifax, Nova Scotia.

ice. They also worked on his balance by running on sand. Marching drills were designed to get Sidney to move quicker and more easily while skating. For strength, O'Brien had Sidney run up, down, and around Citadel Hill, a historic site in Halifax.

Strength training was like the final piece of the puzzle. Combined with his other skills on the ice, strength and speed made Sidney an extra-hot hockey prospect as he prepared to start playing in the major juniors.

QUICK FACT

Trainers, coaches, and fans all seem to agree about what makes Sidney such a great hockey player: great lower-body strength, excellent motor skills, and the ability to see and understand what's going on everywhere on the ice.

CHAPTER TWO

Skating Up the Ladder

Sidney's move back to Canada from the United States allowed him to finish his schooling in his native country, much closer to home. In 2005, he graduated from Harrison Trimble High School in the province of New Brunswick. As he had at Shattuck-St. Mary's, he was able to play hockey while also attending classes—only he did not play for his high school team.

By the summer of 2003, Sidney was sixteen and officially old enough to play in the Canadian major junior league. But he didn't join the Halifax Mooseheads, as he and his parents had hoped would be the case the year before. Instead, Sidney entered the Quebec Major Junior Hockey League (QMJHL) draft. In June 2003, the Rimouski (Quebec) Océanic made Sidney the No. 1 overall pick in the Q draft.

Life in the Major Juniors

Most of the time in organized sports, rookies—those who are first-year players at a certain level of the game—do not get as much playing time as the veteran, or experienced, players. During his rookie season with the Océanic, however, Sidney got plenty of ice time, thanks to his awesome skills. The fact that he was used to "playing up" probably helped coaches make the decision to play him as well. They knew Sidney could handle himself, as well as the puck, even while going up against veterans that were older than he was.

QUICK FACT

Sidney's QMJHL Awards are as follows:

2003–04: Most Valuable Player, Rookie of the Year, Offensive Player of the Year, Offensive Rookie of the Year, Jean Béliveau Trophy for highest scorer

2004–05: Most Valuable Player, Personality of the Year, Offensive Player of the Year, Jean Béliveau Trophy

Sidney calls for the puck during a 2003 Océanic game against the Cape Breton Screaming Eagles of the Canadian Major Juniors.

Sidney racked up 135 points during the 2003–04 season. That total included 54 goals and 81 assists. Among several awards he earned that season was a trophy for being the top scorer. During his second season in the major juniors, Sidney made even more goals and assists. He ended the season with 168 points and again won a bunch of awards, including the scoring title for the second year in a row.

National Championship

Sidney's performance during his first year in the major juniors also earned him a spot on the Canadian Junior Hockey under-20 team at the World Junior Hockey Championships. Team Canada came in second that year, but Sidney managed to become the youngest player to score a goal in tournament history. It was a title he kept until 2012.

Sidney made a repeat appearance at the World Junior tournament in 2005. This time Canada came out on top, winning the championship. Sidney skated away with six goals and three assists over six games in the tournament.

Sidney (*center*) celebrates with teammates after winning the 2005 World Junior Championships against Russia, in Grand Forks, North Dakota.

QUICK FACT

Crosby has been the first overall draft pick four times, for as many separate leagues. He has played only for two of the teams that made him their premiere pick.

Team	League	Year Drafted
Antigonish Bulldogs	Maritime Junior A Hockey League	2002
Rimouski Océanic	Quebec Major Junior Hockey League	2003
Toronto Toros	World Hockey Association	2004
Pittsburgh Penguins	National Hockey League	2005

Going Pro

Sidney wound up not going to college. Instead, he entered the NHL Draft after finishing high school and playing two years with the Océanic. Hockey fans were so sure that Sidney was going to be the top pick

Sidney was the first overall pick in the 2005 NHL Draft. Here, he poses for his first official portrait as a Penguin.

The cover of *Sporting News* magazine announces the arrival of "Sid the Kid" to the Penguins lineup and the NHL.

overall, made by the Pittsburgh Penguins that year, the 2005 draft became known unofficially as the "Sidney Crosby Sweepstakes."

COMPLETE BASEBALL PLAYOFF COVERAGE Shocking Sox change! Cards sharks!

SportingNews

SEE A DIFFERENT GAME

WELCOME BACK, BOYS!

The return of the NHL

USC @ NOTRE DAME
The Irish can win: Our 5-point plan

INSIDE AN NFL LOCKER
(Psst, look behind that TV)

NASCAR
Beware these crash zones

www.sportingnews.com
OCTOBER 21, 2005

Sid the Kid's opening week

PLUS
Todd Bertuzzi, villain or vindicated?

The EXPERTS' Choice
FOOTBALL · BASEBALL · HOOPS · NASCAR

As every hockey fan had expected, Sidney was the first overall pick of the 2005 NHL Draft. The Pittsburgh Penguins chose him to play center for their team. Penguins star Mario Lemieux—the player whose poster had hung on young Sidney's bedroom wall, and to whom Sidney had been compared by the great Wayne Gretzky—took the eighteen-year-old rookie under his wing. Lemieux, who was playing his last season with the Penguins during the 2005–06 season, helped Sidney get used to playing in the NHL as a teammate on the ice. He also made room in his home. Sidney lived with Lemieux and his family during the playing season for the first few years of his NHL career.

Sidney was well on his way to making his dreams of playing professional hockey come true. And there were even more and better things to come.

As Penguins captain in 2005, the legendary Mario Lemieux took Sidney under his wing, both on and off the ice.

Cementing
the Legend

The National Hockey League Draft that took place in the summer of 2005 could not have come at a better time. Disagreements between NHL team owners and league players had caused the entire 2004–05 season to be cancelled. Fans were thrilled when professional hockey games were set to resume in 2005. The fact that the great Sidney Crosby would be joining the league and facing Russian scoring sensation Alexander Ovechkin, who was drafted in 2004, helped to ramp up the excitement level.

By the time he entered the NHL Draft, Sidney Crosby had already become something of a young legend in Canada. His name and skills were well known among hockey fans across North America, including the United States. In time, with a lot of hard work and a burning passion for the game, he would become an absolute superstar, both on and off

Alexander Ovechkin waits for the action to begin again during a game in his rookie season. Ovechkin and Sidney have long been scoring rivals.

Fitting In, Playing Hard

Sidney got a lot of attention right from the first day of training camp in the summer of 2005. The Penguins included a "Crosby Watch" section for each day of practice in the camp updates they gave to the press

QUICK FACT

Crosby's Major NHL Awards
Hart Memorial Trophy for most valuable player (2006–07, 2013–14)
Ted Lindsay Award for most outstanding player, voted on by the league's
Players Association (2006–07, 2012–13, 2013–14)
Art Ross Trophy for top point scorer (2006–07, 2013–14)
Maurice Richard Trophy for top goal scorer (2009–10)

Sidney holds a keep-sake—the puck used to score his first NHL goal—in the locker room after a 2005 game against the Boston Bruins.

and public. Reporters and sportscasters, including a crew from the National Broadcasting Company (NBC), came to practices and tried to get interviews with the star rookie. Sidney did his best not to let the tremendous buzz about his playing get to him. After all, he had an action plan mapped out in his head.

"I'm going to push myself to raise my game as much as I can in camp," he told Shawna Richer of the *Toronto Globe and Mail* newspaper. "It's going to be a challenge to go from junior to the NHL. I feel very fortunate to be in this situation."

QUICK-FACT

Sidney was the first teenager to lead a professional sports team in scoring. He captured that honor during his second year in the NHL when he was nineteen years old, tallying 120 points on 36 goals and 84 assists.

Sidney, seen here during the pre-game playing of the national anthem, made his presence felt right from the start during his rookie season.

Much as he had during his first year with the Océanic, Sidney had a good start with the NHL during his rookie season. He received plenty of playing time and scored 102 points, becoming the youngest NHL player ever to reach one hundred points in a single season.

Taking Charge

According to the official NHL website, a hockey team captain is the only player who can discuss calls that referees make while a game is being played. But a captain is so much more than a player representative. He or she is someone the other players look up to, a leader who encourages teammates to play hard and have a positive attitude.

Before he had even finished his first full season playing pro hockey, Sidney was named an alternate, or assistant, team captain of the Penguins. Alternates act as a team captain when the true captain is injured or otherwise not on the ice. Before the Penguins started the 2007–2008 season, Sidney had been named the team's full-time captain. He was twenty years old and the youngest player ever named captain in the league.

Sidney was well aware of what an honor it was to be named captain, particularly at such a young age. He said it was one of the biggest honors in his professional career.

"You always dream of one day playing in the NHL and you always dream of hoisting that [Stanley] Cup and obviously everyone knows the captain is the one who gets to do that, so I'm hoping one day I have that opportunity."

Little did he know when he made that statement that he and the Penguins would soon experience the thrill of winning the Stanley Cup and being NHL champions.

Lifting the Cup

Another important moment in Sidney's NHL career came at the end of the 2008–09 season.

QUICK FACT

The NHL All Star Game has been played five times between 2005 and 2014. (There were off years because of the Olympics and league lockouts.) Sidney was named to play in each of those five All Star Games but actually took to the ice only in 2007. He missed the other games due to injury.

Sidney plays along the boards behind the net during Game 6 of the 2008 Stanley Cup Finals against the Detroit Red Wings.

Before 2005, the Penguins had been a struggling team that had not been in the play-offs since 2001 and had not won the Stanley Cup since 1992. In 2007, the team made the play-offs, although they did not make it past the quarterfinals. The next year, the Penguins made it to the finals but lost to the Detroit Red Wings. Finally, in the 2009 postseason, Pittsburgh came from behind to beat Detroit in the best-of-seven series to win the Stanley Cup.

No one, including Sidney himself, would say that the Penguins' captain alone brought the Cup back to Pittsburgh. The victory was definitely a team effort, and Sidney sat out most of Game 7 with a knee injury. However, Sidney's influence most certainly made a difference. First, he was responsible for the Penguins' huge turnaround—the fourth largest in NHL history—that led to the team's appearance in the 2007 play-offs. Sidney tied for top scorer in the 2008 play-offs and recorded the most goals scored in the 2009 play-offs.

Hoisting the Stanley Cup, Sidney and the Penguins celebrate their victory over Detroit, in seven games, to become 2009 NHL champs.

The "Golden Goal"

It was late during the last day of play at the 2010 Olympics in Vancouver, Canada. The United States men's ice hockey team had come from behind to tie the gold medal game against Team Canada in the

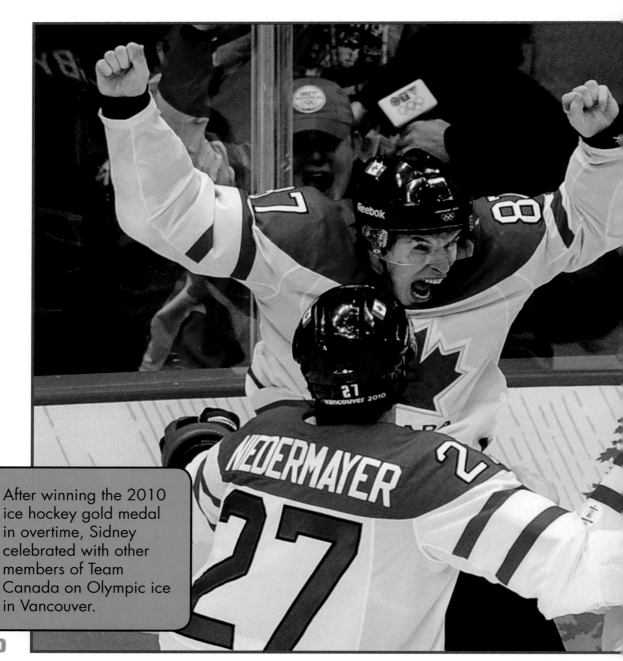

After winning the 2010 ice hockey gold medal in overtime, Sidney celebrated with other members of Team Canada on Olympic ice in Vancouver.

final seconds of regulation play. Going into sudden death overtime, the two teams battled mightily for just over seven minutes.

And then it happened. Sidney, playing for Canada, hit the puck through the U.S. goalie's legs. The arena, which was packed to the rafters with Canadians, erupted with cheers. Sidney had won the game on a shot that has come to be famous as the "Golden Goal."

Sidney, who was an alternate captain on the 2010 Canadian squad, was named captain of the national team during the 2014 Olympic Games. Under his leadership, Team Canada went on to repeat as gold medal champions. But it was arguably his "Golden Goal" in 2010 that put the exclamation mark on Sidney's status as a hockey legend.

Life and Works Off the Ice

It's just another day in a town outside the city of Pittsburgh—that is, until Sidney Crosby rings the doorbell and comes in to chat, bringing season tickets to the Penguins home games with him. Sidney and his teammates have been making deliveries such as this to season-ticket holders for years. True, such visits are part of the Penguins public relations plan, but one gets the feeling that Sidney would be happy to participate even if the team didn't require it. He likes getting out and meeting people.

"Sidney doesn't accept living in a bubble," Sidney's agent, Pat Brisson, told a *Sports Illustrated* reporter in 2013. "Some celebrities,

Fans seek a little face time with "Sid the Kid" Crosby outside Mellon Arena in Pittsburgh. Sidney is a favorite of hockey fans around the globe.

Being Sidney

Here's the lowdown on Sidney Crosby, the person behind the hockey superstar. He loves chocolate chip cookies but has to watch what he eats to stay strong and healthy on the ice. He owns two cars—a Range Rover for Pittsburgh and a Chevy Tahoe for tooling around Halifax—and speaks two languages. One of his favorite hobbies is fishing.

QUICK FACT

Although English is his native language, Sidney made sure to learn French when he played in Quebec. The province is largely French-speaking.

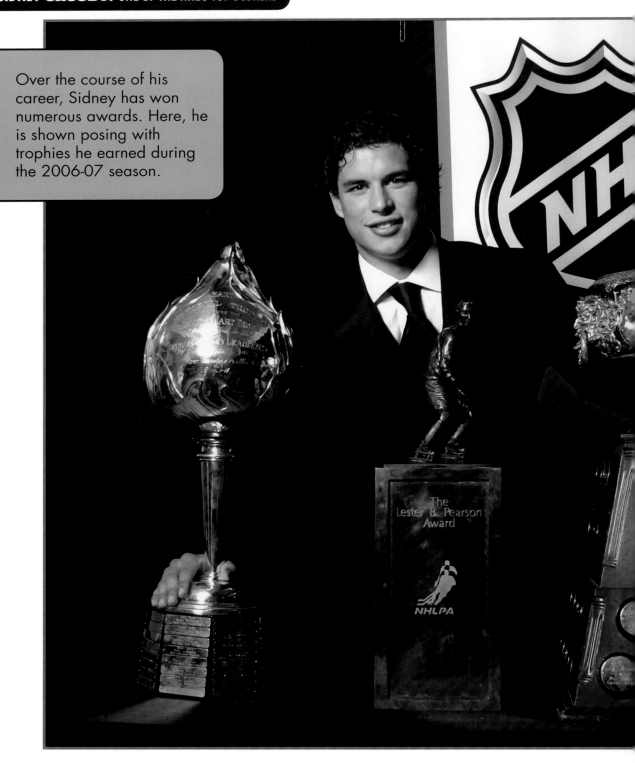

Over the course of his career, Sidney has won numerous awards. Here, he is shown posing with trophies he earned during the 2006-07 season.

The Lester B. Pearson Award

NHLPA

Many athletes are superstitious. They find comfort in doing things a certain way, saying that it brings them luck and helps them to win. Sidney is no exception. Among his reported game-day rituals are:

- Being the only one who can tape his stick, or touch it after it's taped

- Calling his mom before games

- Eating in the same restaurant while playing away games in other cities

- Having certain teammates sit to the left and right of him when he eats

A Soft Spot for Kids

Even as a child, Sidney had a kind streak. The assistant principal of his junior high school remembers that as a student, Sidney went out of his way to be nice to children in the school's learning center, as well as those with special needs. Caring about what happens to youngsters is still very much on the mind of "Sid the Kid." He visits sick kids in Pittsburgh and Halifax-area hospitals fairly often. A suite in the Penguins' home sports arena is often

Sidney is active in many charitable causes. Here, he poses for the NHL's Hockey Fights Cancer initiative.

reserved by Sidney so that sick or underserved children and their families can come watch a game.

To help support his charity work, Sidney started the Sidney Crosby Foundation in 2009. Based in Nova Scotia, Canada, the foundation focuses mainly on organizations that help children. Charities that have benefited from foundation funds, and with which Sidney has personally worked, include Make-a-Wish, Big Brothers/Big Sisters, and the Special Olympics, among many others.

QUICK FACT

When police returned his stolen jersey from the 2005 World Junior Hockey Championships, Sidney decided to auction it off instead of keeping it. He gave the money raised to youth hockey charities and organizations helping those affected by the December 2004 tsunami in South Asia.

Hockey for All

Sidney also actively participates in a number of programs that benefit kids who are interested in playing hockey. For instance, he has acted as a spokesperson for Timbits Minor Hockey—the same program in which he started playing organized hockey when he was five years old.

Another program, Little Penguins Learn to Play Hockey, was Sidney's idea. To help Pittsburgh-area parents afford getting their children started playing the sport, he convinced the Penguins' management, shoe manufacturer Reebok, and the Dick's Sporting Goods chain of stores to help him fund the program. There is a fee to join the program, but that covers lessons and rink time. Equipment for each participant, from skates and sticks to helmets and pads, is provided for free.

QUICK FACT

Sidney made an appearance in two movies, 2008's *Pond Hockey* and the comedy *She's Out of My League*, which was released in 2010.

Sidney's popularity has won him many endorsement deals. Here, he is shown speaking to the media during a Reebok marketing event in 2007.

Money Matters

One reason Sidney can afford to help so many people is that he is well paid for his job. In 2012, the Penguins signed him to a contract extension that will pay him $104.4 million over the course of twelve years playing for the team. Added to his player's salary are endorsement deals he has made with several companies, including Gatorade, Tim Horton's, and Bell Canada. His deal with Reebok, which pays him $1.4 million, includes a clothing line, SC87, named using Sidney's initials and his hockey jersey number.

Although the money certainly is nice, it isn't the reason Sidney plays hockey. He plays simply because he enjoys it. Plus, he's very good at it and will only get better the more he practices and plays. As Troy Crosby told *Sports Illustrated* early in his son's career, "He never wanted to be the next Wayne Gretzky or the next Mario Lemieux. He wants to be Sidney Crosby. He's comfortable with who he is. He's not just playing hockey. He's playing to be the best he can be."

TIMELINE

August 8, 1987   Sidney Patrick Crosby is born.

1990   Sidney is already skating at the age of three.

1994   Gives first newspaper interview.

2002–03   Attends Shattuck-St. Mary's school in Minnesota.

June 2003   Drafted by the Rimouski Océanic of the Quebec Major Junior Hockey League.

August 2003   Plays in the under-18 World Junior Championships.

December 18, 2004   Wins his first gold medal in the juniors while playing for Team Canada in the under-20 World Junior Championships.

July 30, 2005   Chosen as the number one overall pick in that year's NHL Entry Draft.

December 2005   Named an alternate captain of the Pittsburgh Penguins.

April 2006   Becomes the youngest rookie to score one hundred NHL points in a single season.

2007   Made full-time captain of the Penguins.

January 2007   Becomes the youngest NHL player ever to start in an All Star Game.

May 2008   Sidney and the Penguins reach the finals of the NHL Stanley Cup Championships, losing to the Detroit Red Wings.

June 12, 2009   The Penguins win the Stanley Cup.

2010   Key member of the Canadian men's hockey team at the 2010 Olympic Winter Games in Vancouver.

February 28, 2010   Scores the "Golden Goal" that clinches Canada's victory in the 2010 Olympics men's ice hockey final.

June 28, 2012   Signs a twelve-year contract extension, worth millions of dollars, with the Penguins.

2014   Captains the Canadian Olympic men's hockey team, which takes home the gold medal at the Winter Games in Sochi, Russia.

Bobby Hull (1939–), nicknamed "the Golden Jet," was known for lightning-fast speed on the ice and a slapshot that was clocked at 120 mph (193 kph). Hull played twenty-three years in the NHL, mainly for the Chicago Blackhawks. He was the first player to score more than fifty goals in a single season.

Wayne Gretzky (1961–) is considered by many to be the greatest hockey player of all time. He played for the Edmonton Oilers and Los Angeles Kings, and he is the holder of more than sixty NHL records. Gretzky himself predicted that Sidney Crosby would break many of those records.

Mark Messier (1961–) was one of the all-time greatest scorers in NHL history, as well as a two-time league MVP. The first team captain to lead two teams (the Oilers and the New York Rangers) to Stanley Cup victories, Messier is considered one of the game's great leaders.

Mario Lemieux (1965–) was the top NHL scorer in six different seasons with the Pittsburgh Penguins. In 2000, he came out of retirement to play again with the team, only this time as part-owner. Lemieux was inducted into the Hockey Hall of Fame in 1997.

Jagr Jaromir (1972–), born in Czechoslovakia (now the Czech Republic), was on the Czech national team that won Olympic gold—the country's first gold ever—in 1998. He also helped the Penguins win the Stanley Cup in 1991 and 1992.

Jenny Potter (1979–) is one of the most honored players in U.S. women's hockey. A stellar college player, she has won medals at four consecutive Olympic games (1998, 2002, 2006, 2010) as part of the U.S. women's national hockey team.

Alexander Ovechkin (1985–) was as hot a junior prospect in Russia as Sidney was in Canada. He has been named the NHL MVP three times (2008, 2009, 2013) and frequently challenges Sidney for the title of top scorer in the league.

GLOSSARY

alternate Someone or something that is available to take the place of an original, every once in a while.

amateur Used to describe someone who does something for fun, not as a job.

draft A system for or act of selecting individuals from a group.

endorsement Money earned from a product recommendation for a product or service.

extension An increase in time allowed under agreement, such as a contract.

goal The act of getting a ball or puck into the area of a playing field that results in a score.

impressive Having the power to excite or gain a lot of attention.

jersey A loose shirt worn by a member of a sports team as part of a uniform.

legend A famous or important person who is known for doing something extremely well.

motor skills The ability to move muscles in such a way to complete tasks or perform well in sports.

play-offs A series of games that is played after the end of the regular season in order to decide which player or team is the champion.

puck A rubber disk used in ice hockey.

rookie A first-year player in a professional sport.

slapshot A hockey shot that is made by swinging your stick with a lot of force.

tournament A sports competition that involves many players or teams and usually continues for at least several days.

Books

Biskup, Agnieszka. *Hockey: How It Works*. Mankato, MN: Capstone Press, 2010.

Burns, Kylie. *Superstars! Sidney Crosby*. New York, NY: Crabtree Publishing Co., 2012.

Frederick, Shane. *Side-by-Side Hockey Stars: Comparing Pro Hockey's Greatest Players*. North Mankato, MN: Capstone Press, 2014.

Frederick, Shane. *Six Degrees of Sidney Crosby: Connecting Hockey Stars*. North Mankato, MN: Capstone Press, 2015.

Gitlin, Marty. *Hockey* (Best Sport Ever). Minneapolis, MN: ABDO Publishing Company, 2012.

Johnstone, Robb. *Hockey*. New York, NY: Weigl Publishers, 2010.

Killcoyne, Hope Lourie. *Hockey and Its Greatest Players* (Inside Sports). New York, NY: Rosen Publishing, 2015.

Labrecque, Ellen. *The World's Greatest Athletes: Ice Kings*. Mankato, MN: The Child's World Publishing, 2014.

McMahon, Dave. *Sidney Crosby: Hockey's Golden Boy*. Fort Wayne, IN: Sportszone Publishing, 2011.

Roza, Greg. *Today's Sports Greats: Sidney Crosby*. New York, NY: Rosen Publishing, 2011.

Shea, Therese. *Greatest Sports Heroes: Hockey Stars*. New York, NY: Children's Press, 2007.

Siemasz, Greg. *Hockey* (Winter Sports). Chicago, IL: Raintree, 2014.

Stewart, Mark, and Mike Kennedy. *Score! The Action and Artistry of Hockey's Magnificent Moment*. Minneapolis, MN: Millbrook Press, 2013. Kindle ed.

Wilner, Barry. *Wayne Gretzky: Hockey's "The Great One"* (Legendary Athletes). Minneapolis, MN: ABDO Publishing Company, 2014.

Winters, Jaime. *Center Ice: The Stanley Cup* (Hockey Source). St. Catharines, ON: Crabtree Publishing Company, 2014.

Websites

Because of the changing nature of Internet links, Rosen Publishing has developed an online list of websites related to the subject of this book. This site is updated regularly. Please use this link to access the list:

http://www.rosenlinks.com/LLS/Cros

INDEX

R

Richer, Shawna, 23
Rimouski Océanic (QMJHL),
   14–16, 17, 25

S

Shattuck-St. Mary's boarding
   school, 10, 12, 14
She's Out of My League, 37
Sidney Crosby Foundation, 37
Special Olympics, 37
Stanley Cup, 26, 28
superstition rituals, 35

T

team captain, role of, 25
Timbits Minor Hockey program,
   9, 37

U

Under 18 World Junior
   Championships, 10

W

World Junior Hockey
   Championships, 16, 37